Comprehension 3 Teachers' Handbook

Contents

Part one

Part two

UNIVERSITY OF LEICESTER
SCHOOL OF EDUCATION

PART ONE

Introduction

To develop as effective readers, pupils should be taught to:
- read accurately, fluently and with understanding;
- understand and respond to the texts they read;
- read, analyse, and evaluate a wide range of texts, including literature from the English literary heritage and from other cultures and traditions.
(Revised National Curriculum for English in England and Wales, General requirements for English, 1995)

Learning to read accurately and with discrimination becomes increasingly important as pupils move through their education... [Pupils] should be helped to develop their own tastes in imaginative literature and non-fiction and at the same time to gain confidence in writing and speaking about them... The importance of meaning should be stressed at all stages...
(Scottish 5-14 English Language Curriculum, June 1991)

Pupils should develop the ability to read, understand and engage with various types of text for enjoyment and learning.
(Northern Ireland Curriculum, 1990)

The reading skills described above are those which every teacher of English aims to foster and it is these skills that the Key Comprehension series targets.

Key Comprehension comprises three Pupils' Books and three accompanying Teachers' Handbooks, aimed at Key Stage 1 / Primary 3, Lower Key Stage 2 / Primary 4-5 and Upper Key Stage 2 / Primary 6-7. The series helps to prepare pupils for the Reading Comprehension components of the national Standard Assessment Tasks / National Tests (Scotland). The series may also be used to prepare pupils for the comprehension components of 11+ entry tests in English to grammar schools and independent schools.

Book 1 prepares pupils in Year 2 for Reading Comprehension Tests at Key Stage 1 / pupils in Primary 3 for the National Tests for infants. It is targeted at National Curriculum Levels 2-4, Scottish 5-14 Curriculum Level A and Northen Ireland Curriculum Levels 1-3.

Book 2 is aimed at pupils in Years 3 and 4 / Primary 4-5 and is targeted at National Curriculum Levels 3-5 / Scottish 5-14 Curriculum Levels B-C and Northen Ireland Curriculum Levels 2-4.

Book 3 prepares pupils in Years 5 and 6 for the Reading Comprehension Tests at Key Stage 2 / pupils in Primary 6-7 for the National Tests for juniors. It is targeted at National Curriculum Levels 3-6; Scottish 5-14 Curriculum Levels C-D; and Northen Ireland Curriculum Levels 3-5.

Structure and components

Key Comprehension Book 3 contains thirty self-contained Units of work. Each Unit consists of a short passage of text followed by a series of questions which test the children's understanding of the text.

The texts are taken from a wide range of sources, and are lively and stimulating. Care has been taken to reflect the pupils' own experience and to engage their interest. In accordance with Curriculum guidelines, the genres represented include modern and well-established children's fiction, fables, myths, information texts, and transactional material.

The questions are designed to encourage close and accurate reading of the texts and to foster an understanding of implicit as well as explicit meaning. The activities gradually become more demanding as the book progresses. The pupils' ability to skim and to scan, to order and to summarise, to pinpoint and to synthesise information is thus developed throughout the book.

For each Unit, the Teachers' Handbook provides answers to the questions, a breakdown of the comprehension skills tested in the activity, a suggested marks scheme and a range of ideas for extension work. These extension activities are often open-ended and offer a range of written assignments in a variety of genres, comprehension questions of greater complexity, and related language work.

The Teachers' Handbook also contains a commentary on the range of reading strategies that are needed to develop comprehension skills, National Curricula correlation information, pupil and class record sheets and a Bibliography containing details of the sources of texts for further reading.

How to use Key Comprehension

Units are arranged in order of gradually increasing difficulty and, generally speaking, are intended to be tackled in the order arranged. However, each Unit is self-contained to allow flexibility so teachers may choose to take some Units out of order if a particular topic, genre or question form is relevant to current class work.

Teachers will find that some children who are confident, independent readers are happy to tackle the Units with the minimum of teacher intervention. Others, however, will need considerable support and guidance before this stage is reached. Most children will benefit if the teacher talks through the activity first and explains exactly what they are being asked to do. If the children's own reading is hesitant, they will be helped by the teacher's reading the passage to them and thereby arousing their attention and interest.

Although a prolonged discussion at the end of the reading would be inappropriate, it is a good opportunity to deal with questions, pose a few tactical ones in anticipation of the printed ones that follow and perhaps discuss relevant aspects of the illustrations. When the children are comfortable with the passage, it can be helpful if the text is "put back together again" by being read aloud a second time.

The teacher may then wish to read through the questions with the children and discuss answers. In this informal atmosphere, the teacher is able to encourage and to prompt, and to praise warmly when thoughtful answers (firmly based on the text) are given. Children must be encouraged to pay close attention to the exact wording of the question, and to consider it in its entirety before attempting an answer. Teachers can also help children search the text for the answer, and gently dismiss hopefully inventive responses.

As their confidence grows, children will be happy working together in pairs and in groups, reading the passage and questions themselves. Teachers will need to be on hand to support, guide and focus attention when appropriate. Collaborative activities can be very supportive when the members are well matched and each contributes thoughtfully, but teachers need to be vigilant to spot those who are taking without giving, and simply copying the answers down.

Sequencing, cloze and multiple choice activities lend themselves easily to consensus decisions, and can be self-marked by the group from answers given in the Teachers' Handbook. This self-marking can be a learning activity too if the group returns to the text to establish the validity of the given answer where the group had made a wrong decision. Units where answers have to be given in the pupils' own words are sometimes less satisfactory as collaborative activities unless the children are sophisticated enough to benefit from the discussion and are happy to express themselves on paper independently. Pupils will find it more difficult to assess their own answer here by comparison with the suggested answers because wording may vary considerably.

The Teachers' Handbook allocates a full page to each Unit, and provides suggested answers and extension activities. Teachers may wish to give children a photocopy the relevant page and allow children to check their own work alongside the suggested answers and then go on to work on the extension activities provided on the same sheet.

Key Comprehension can be used to give children an opportunity to work in controlled conditions from time to time in preparation for the National Curriculum Reading Comprehension tests (England and Wales, Northern Ireland) and 5-14 National Tests (Scotland). Children unused to working on their own and in silence can be disadvantaged and unnecessarily stressed during such unfamiliar formal tests. Units from Key Comprehension can be used for individual silent practice, and pupils can become accustomed to the rules of "no conferring" and "no asking questions". They can also become familiar with working against the clock if the practice is timed.

Lastly, the Units form a useful basis for homework assignments where parental involvement can be guided and encouraged.

Reading comprehension terminology

Reading strategies

Skimming, scanning and detailed reading are essential strategies for effective information retrieval and to encourage full understanding and exploration of texts. All three strategies are developed during the course of Key Comprehension Book 3.

Skimming and scanning are terms much in use since the advent of the National Curricula. They are often used rather vaguely but are, in fact, two distinct reading strategies.

Skimming

Skimming involves reading swiftly through text in order to register the general outline (the gist) and omitting the detail. This gives the reader an overview of the material and an idea of where in the text, roughly, to find passages for closer reading later.

Scanning

Scanning involves rapid but focused reading of text, in order to locate specific information, e.g. looking for particular details such as dates, names, certain types of words, and so on.

Detailed reading

Detailed reading involves reading text slowly and accurately in order to reflect upon the structure, purpose, content and tone of the text. The reader reads attentively listening carefully to what the writer is saying.

When tackling the thirty Units in Book 3, pupils will have to employ skimming, scanning and detailed reading techniques on a regular basis. The questions direct pupils back to the text in order to find the answers. Pupils need to be told that referring back to the text is expected (*and is not cheating!*). Reading Comprehension is not a memory test but an exercise in information retrieval and understanding.

Comprehension skills: literal, deductive inferential and evaluative understanding

Key Comprehension Book 3 develops pupils' understanding of what they have read at several levels. As would be expected for upper juniors, the questions in the Units require deductive, inferential and evaluative understanding as well as literal understanding. These questions are designed to encourage pupils to read between the lines and interpret what they have read. A wide variety of questionsis used to elicit a full range of responses requiring all these types of understanding.

Literal

Literal responses demonstrate the ability to understand the surface meaning of a text and to select information accurately from the text in answer to a question.
For example:

Question	How old was Fern? (Unit 7)
Answer	*Fern was eight years old.*

Deductive

Deductive responses demonstrate the ability to reach a logical conclusion by drawing on personal experience from beyond the immediate context of the passage.
For example:

Question	Mr Patel was "something of an expert" at arranging firework displays. What does this mean? (Unit 15)
Answer	*This means that he was very good at arranging firework displays.*

Inferential

Inferential responses demonstrate the ability to reach a logical conclusion on the basis of information given.
For example:

Question	What was it that stopped Lucy whimpering? (Unit 12)
Answer	Lucy stopped whimpering when she heard the sound of the door opening in her dream.

Evaluative

Evaluative responses demonstrate the ability to appraise, to form judgements and to weigh the evidence and its implications.
For example:

Question	Do you think Mrs Peach is a good or a bad mother? Why? (Unit 30)
Answer	*(A personal response is required here.)*

Range of question forms

The following chart summarises the range of question forms used in each Unit of work in Key Comprehension Book 3.

	sentence completion	true/false	multiple choice	answering in own words
UNIT 1			•	
UNIT 2	•			
UNIT 3		•		•
UNIT 4			•	
UNIT 5				•
UNIT 6		•		
UNIT 7				•
UNIT 8				•
UNIT 9				•
UNIT 10		•		•
UNIT 11				•
UNIT 12				•
UNIT 13		•		
UNIT 14			•	
UNIT 15				•
UNIT 16				•
UNIT 17		•		
UNIT 18				•
UNIT 19				•
UNIT 20		•		
UNIT 21				•
UNIT 22				•
UNIT 23				•
UNIT 24				•
UNIT 25				•
UNIT 26				•
UNIT 27				•
UNIT 28				•
UNIT 29				•
UNIT 30				•

Teaching comprehension skills

The National Curricula, and good teaching practice, enshrine the belief that comprehension skills can be taught:

> To develop as effective readers, pupils should be taught to:
> - read accurately, fluently and with understanding;
> - understand and respond to the texts they read
> *(English in the National Curriculum, England and Wales, general requirements for English, p.2)*

> The importance of meaning should be stressed at all stages. The activity of reading should take place, wherever possible, in an appropriate context, and it should be concerned with the gaining of meaning from a suitable text.
> *(English Language 5-14, introduction to Reading Programme of Study, p.36)*

> Pupils should develop the ability to read, understand and engage with various types of text for enjoyment and learning.
> *(Northern Ireland Curriculum, Introduction to AT2: Reading, p.35)*

So how can such relatively sophisticated skills be taught and developed?

What exactly can the teacher in the classroom do?

It is helpful to realise that understanding a text and answering accurately questions based on it involve a cluster of acquired skills:

1 detailed reading
2 search reading (skimming and scanning)
3 retrieval (identification and selection)
4 communication (speaking/writing)

Let us look more closely at each of these.

1 Development of detailed reading skills

Detailed reading (without skipping) gives the reader a clear grasp of the narrative. It enables the reader to know what the text is about, although more than one reading may be necessary to unlock the meaning fully.

Children can be helped to develop their detailed reading skills by answering questions, both orally and on paper, as teachers have long known. In the early stages a great deal of reading through the passages in the Units with the pupils may well be necessary. Dialogue and discussion, reading and talking about what is being read, help to focus a child's attention on the meaning of the words he or she may well have been reading fluently but without engagement. Children can be prompted by a supportive teacher to return to the text just read to find the right answer to a question. Such questioning and this textual referral help to encourage focused, attentive and reflective reading.

It will also be useful to return to the text after the written answers have been completed to establish why some answers were incorrect or incomplete.

Detailed reading of the text is the key to understanding it. Needless to say, detailed reading of the questions is also very important.

2 Development of search reading skills (skimming and scanning)

When a child has an over-view of a text, search reading skills are needed to locate quickly information required to answer a question. The child will know that the information is there somewhere but will need to be able to read through quickly to find it (skimming) and scrutinise when found (scanning).

The ability to skim over the surface of a text in search of information is a skill that children will probably not develop for themselves without encouragement. Many children, even at secondary level, have only one reading speed when tackling printed text.

Children can be encouraged to skim familiar texts by having small-group or whole-class *skimming races*. The teacher pose challenges such as "Find the place where it says in the passage that David has blue eyes". Winners have to put a finger on the right place in the text. It is wise to allow several children to raise their other hand triumphantly but then to intervene and show the rest before embarking on another search.

Scanning races yield information as well as location. The challenge above would be re-phrased as "Find the place in the passage where it tells us what colour David's eyes are". Winners would have to be able to locate the place in the text and retrieve the information. Children who simply remember the information get no credit here! The exercise is to locate the information with maximum speed.

3 Development of retrieval skills

The questions in the Key Comprehension series have been carefully devised to test (in a variety of forms) literal, deductive, inferential, and evaluative understanding.

Questions testing *literal* understanding will simply require children to retrieve the relevant information from the text. The clues will be lying on the surface of the text. Once children have become used to referring back to the text for the information they need (and not relying on memory alone and not making up fanciful answers), this type of question should present no great difficulties. Children should enjoy locating and retrieving the answer.

Retrieving implicit meaning by *deduction* or *inference* is much more difficult, and children need to be helped to read between the lines. Questions targeting implicit meaning will be phrased along these lines: "How do you know that Sarah is the eldest child in the family?"; "Why do you think Tom feels so sad?" Children will be helped by gentle support here as they look for hidden clues. It does help to think of deductive and inferential retrieval skills as detective work! Plenty of practice is offered in Key Comprehension and children will gain much by working in pairs and small groups and exchanging their ideas as they discuss the text. Such discussions can be monitored by the teacher who can steer them away from unprofitable avenues and aim them in the right direction with some judicious questions. If children later have access to the answers in the Teachers' Handbook, they can see for themselves points in the given answers that they may have overlooked.

Occasionally *evaluative* answers are invited, requiring children to express an opinion which must be supported by close reference to the textual evidence. Such questions are open-ended and all pupils will have something valid to say. More able pupils will have the opportunity to marshal a cogent argument and to develop a view.

Children will meet a wide variety of question forms in the Units and it can be helpful to alert them to the demands each form presents.

In *cloze* activities, children should be reminded that they need to read right to the end of the sentence before supplying the missing word. Some children attempt to fill the gap as soon as they reach it, not realising that the sentence as a whole provides the necessary contextual clues.

In *sequencing* activities, children need to be assured that there is one best ordering of the parts within the completed whole. They can be guided to spot sequential clues such as "Begin by ...", "next" and "finally", for example. They must make a logical and not a random choice in sequencing.

In *sentence completion*, what is added must fit syntactically and must complete the sense of the sentence satisfactorily. The completed sentence must be accurate when cross-referenced with the text. The temptation must be resisted to add any random ending that happens to occur to the child.

Children should be warned that *True/False* activities may well lay traps for the unwary reader. Slight but significant variations of wording may render one choice unacceptable although very close to the truth. Children can be warned not to fall into the trap.

Multiple choice. Here again, distracters may well be included that are very nearly the answer required. Great vigilance is necessary and all the possible choices should be considered carefully before a decision is made. It can be helpful to eliminate any obviously incorrect statements and then to concentrate on choosing the right answer from the statements that remain.

When children are *answering in their own words*, they should be reminded not to lift material straight from the passage but to answer the question clearly in their own way. Sometimes there is more than one point to be made. Children should make sure they have included all that is relevant in their answer.

4 Developing communication skills.

Whether children discuss a reading comprehension or write their answers in carefully controlled conditions, they are developing communication skills. In pair work and in small group discussions, ideas should be shared courteously and productively, and the quality of the reading comprehension shown can be assessed by the monitoring teacher.

Answering reading comprehension questions by writing the answers can be a very challenging exercise for children with limited writing skills. It is for this reason that a variety of approaches is used to familiarise them with the kinds of structures useful when they come to answer questions in their own words.

Sometimes they are asked to copy out and complete a sentence (cloze and sentence completion); sometimes they have to select and write out a sentence from a pair or group in answer to a question (true/false, multiple choice); sometimes they have to write out sentences and captions in a logical order (sequencing). As the series progresses, they are expected to answer more questions in their own words, although more supportive exercises (from the writing point of view) are interspersed with these throughout the series.

Reading comprehension is traditionally tested by the writing of answers to questions. The development of writing skills will be encouraged not only by answering the questions in each of the Units but also by attempting the many varied extension activities in the Teachers' Book.

Teaching reading comprehension skills is an on-going classroom activity not, of course, confined to the English lesson. Such skills are vital if our children are to be enabled as enthusiastic, independent and reflective readers, as we would wish each one of them to be.

Key Comprehension and the National Curricula

Key Comprehension and National Curricula tests

Teachers may wish to use Key Comprehension Units formally in the classroom as preparation for National Curriculum Reading Comprehension tests (England and Wales, Northern Ireland) and 5-14 National Tests (Scotland).

Key Comprehension is a flexible resource and the Units may usefully be worked in controlled conditions as children become more confident about working individually and independently of teacher intervention. For some children, who are used only to working in pairs or groups, the experience of formally conducted tests can be a frightening one. Timed activities or conventions forbidding them to ask for help can be unfamiliar and bewildering.

Key Comprehension offers the opportunity of controlled practice in a supportive environment where the experience can be talked through beforehand and discussed afterwards. The overall task will gradually become familiar and the conventions understood. Children will be better prepared for formal tests if they have been given the opportunity from time to time of writing and working independently and quietly.

National Curriculum for England and Wales

The Key Stage 2 Programme of Study indicates three main areas of importance in Reading. These areas are: Range of reading, Key skills and Standard English and Language study. Key Comprehension is directed at nurturing skills of reading a range of texts with fluency, accuracy and understanding, and thus provides support for the Curriculum.

The following chart draws on key phrases and concepts from the Reading Programme of Study for Key Stage 2, as set out in English in the National Curriculum (HMSO 1995).

PROGRAMME OF STUDY REFERENCE	KEY COMPREHENSION BOOK 3
Range of reading **1a** Pupils should be encouraged to develop as enthusiastic, independent and reflective readers. Their reading should be developed through the use of progressively more challenging and demanding texts.	Texts chosen are interesting and motivating. Texts progress gradually in difficulty.
1c Pupils' reading should include texts: with challenging subject matter; with complex structures; that include figurative language; with a variety of structural features	Texts include a variety of styles, structures and genres; activities include questions which focus specifically on figurative language
1d The literature read should include: modern fiction, established fiction, poetry, texts from a variety of cultures, myths and legends.	Texts include recent, established and traditional children's fiction, poems, fables, information texts and transactional texts.
Key skills **2b** Pupils should be taught to consider in detail the quality and depth of what they have read. They should be taught to use inference and deduction. They should be taught to evaluate the texts they have read and refer to relevant passages to support their opinions.	Activities target reading texts for understanding; comprehension questions require literal, deductive, inferential and evaluative responses; questions require pupils to refer back to the text to identify and retrieve information.
2c Pupils should be given opportunities to read for different purposes, using skimming and scanning to obtain specific information.	Activities require pupils to use skimming and scanning techniques to find information needed to answer questions.
Standard English and Language Study Pupils should be introduced to the features of different types of text. They should be encouraged to develop their understanding of the structure, vocabulary and grammar of Standard English.	Texts include a variety of styles, structures and genres. Comprehension questions ask for answers written in complete sentences to encourage development of appropriate Standard English writing in a formal context.

English Language 5-14 Curriculum (Scotland)

Key Comprehension encourage children to read for meaning and with understanding and thus supports the 5-14 Curriculum.

The following chart draws on key phrases and concepts from the reading Attainment Targets and Programme of Study for Levels C-D, as set out in English Language 5-14 (1991).

PROGRAMME OF STUDY REFERENCE	KEY COMPREHENSION BOOK 3
AT Strand **Reading to reflect on the writer's ideas and craft** **Level C** Read a variety of straightforward texts, and in discussion and writing show that they understand the main and supporting ideas and can draw conclusions from the text where appropriate.	Key Comprehension provides a structured framework for written comprehension tasks.
Level D Read a variety of straightforward texts, and in discussion and writing show that they understand the gist of the text, its main ideas and/or feelings and can obtain particular information.	Extension activities in the Teachers' Handbook offer suggestions for follow-up work including discussion ideas and open-ended activities. Notes in the Teachers' Handbook identify the types of understanding tested by each question.
(Introduction to PoS) Learning to read accurately and with discrimination becomes increasingly important as pupils move through their education. The importance of meaning should be stressed at all stages.	Key Comprehension activities focus on developing reading with understanding.
As texts become more complex and various in form, the teacher needs to deploy a widening range of techniques such as sequencing, prediction, cloze procedure, evaluating the text, making deductions, marking text, comparing and contrasting different texts.	A variety of comprehension question forms and techniques is used including sequencing, cloze procedure, literal, inferential, deductive and evaluative question forms.
Reading activities should demand that pupils show an overall grasp of a text, an understanding of specific details and how they contribute to the whole, make inferences, supply supporting evidence.	Questions require pupils to read closely and use skimming and scanning techniques to retrieve specific information.
In teaching reading through all stages, in ways appropriate to pupils' ages and attainment, the teacher can focus on texts: *before reading,* by priming pupils for the task, for example by alerting them to unfamiliar content or ideas; by directing them into the task; *during and after reading,*	Texts increase in difficulty gradually. Teachers' Handbook suggests ways of introducing the formal comprehension activities, how to encourage the children to tackle the tasks and how to follow up the work.
by providing questions which ask for literal, inferential and evaluative responses; by asking them to demonstrate understanding by doing or speaking; by asking readers to use the text as a model for their own writing.	Activities include literal, inferential and evaluative questions designed to develop comprehension skills.

Northern Ireland Curriculum for English

The Northern Ireland curriculum states that: "Pupils should develop the ability to read, understand and engage with various types of text for enjoyment and learning" (Attainment Target 2: Reading).

Key Comprehension supports this aim by targeting reading for understanding using a wide range of texts and question types.

The following chart draws on key phrases and cncepts from the Reading Programme of Study for Key Stage 2 as set out in the Northern Ireland Curriculum English document (1990).

PROGRAMME OF STUDY REFERENCE	KEY COMPREHENSION BOOK 3
Level 2a read with some independence, concentration and understanding, a range of texts for enjoyment and learning	Understanding of a range of interesting and enjoyable texts is tested through a structured comprehension programme.
2d listen to and read stories, poems and other materials and engage with them in a variety of ways	Formal comprehension activities in the Pupil's Book test literal, deductive, inferential and evaluative comprehension. Varied extension ideas are suggested in the Teachers' Handbook including discussion points and open-ended activities.
Level 3a read silently, with concentration sufficient to the task, a range of texts for enjoyment and learning	Questions requiring literal, deductive, inferential and evaluative responses are included.
3d demonstrate in talking about their reading, that they are beginning to use text evidence, inference and deduction to explore and appreciate meanings	Question types are fully referenced in Teachers' Handbook.
Level 4b demonstrate, in talking and writing that they are using evidence, inference and deduction from the text to explore and appreciate meanings	Questions require pupils to locate specific details in texts, to interpret what they have read and to demonstrate their understanding.
5b demonstrate that they are developing their own views and responses and can support them by reference to details in the text	Evaluative questions and extension activities prompt a personal response.

Bibliography

The texts used in Key Comprehension Book 3 are taken from the following sources:

Recent and established fiction

The frantic phantom, Norman Hunter, The Bodley Head (Unit 1)
The kingdom by the sea, Robert Westall, Methuen & Co. (Unit 4)
Charlotte's web, E. B. White, Hamish Hamilton Ltd (Unit 7)
"A Martian comes to stay", Penelope Lively from *A sackful of stories for Eight Year Olds*
    ed. P. Thomson, Corgi Books (Unit 8)
Tom's midnight garden, Philippa Pearce, Oxford University Press (Unit 11)
The Iron Woman, Ted Hughes, Faber & Faber (Unit 12)
Sumitra's story, R. Smith, Pan Macmillan Ltd (Unit 15)
Black Beauty, Anna Sewell, Armada Books (Unit 16)
The chicken gave it to me, Anne Fine, Reed Consumer Books (Unit 19)
The Borrowers by Mary Norton, Puffin Books(Unit 21)
Cider with Rosie, Laurie Lee, Longman (Unit 23)
The railway children, E. Nesbit, Puffin Books (Unit 24)
Rosie and the Boredom Eater, Helen Cresswell, William Heinemann Ltd (Unit 25)
Stig of the dump, Clive King, Kestrel Books (Unit 27)
I am David, Anna Holm, Methuen & Co. (Unit 28)
The White Horse Gang, Nina Bawden, Victor Gollancz Ltd (Unit 30)

Fables

The woman, the boy and the lion, from *New Caribbean Junior Reader 5*, Ginn (Unit 10)

Poems

"A thoroughly modern Grandmama" by Moira Andrew from *All in the family*, ed. John Foster,
    Oxford University Press (Unit 2)
"Remember me?" by Ray Mather from *New Caribbean Junior Reader 5*, Ginn (Unit 5)
"The bully asleep" by John Walsh from *The Puffin Book of children's twentieth century verse*
    (Unit 18)
"The longest journey in the world" by Michael Rosen from *Touchstones* ed. Michael & Pete
    Benton, Hodder & Stoughton (Unit 22)

Information texts

Nature detectives: Insects, Anita Garner, Franklin Watts (Unit 3)
The Dorling Kindersley Illustrated Encyclopedia (Unit 6)
Twenty inventors, Jacqueline Dineen, Wayland Publishers Ltd (Unit 9)
Animal kingdom, Malcolm Penny, Wayland Publishers Ltd (Unit 13)
Lady with a lamp, Cyril Davey, The Lutterworth Press (Unit 14)
The cloth of emperors, adapted from *New Caribbean Junior Reader 4*, Ginn (Unit 17)
Treasure hunting, Ian Elliott Shircore, Macdonald Educational Books (Unit 20)
"Hop-scotch tots", from *The Leader*, 26 October 1994, Exmouth and Budleigh Salterton
    (local newspaper) (Unit 26)
Noise, compiled from various sources (Unit 29)

Record keeping

Class record sheet

The Class record sheet on page 16 gives an overall picture of the marks gained in each Unit by every pupil in the class.

Pupil record sheet

The Pupil record sheet on page 17 can be used to record in detail each pupil's performance in reading comprehension.

    The questions set in each Unit are arranged to highlight the type of reading comprehension tested. Question numbers appear in the top part of each rectangle leaving space in the lower part to indicate that each question has been attempted by the pupil.

    The right hand column provides space to record the total mark out of 15 gained in each Unit.

Class record sheet

READING COMPREHENSION

CLASS: YEAR: TEACHER:

UNITS (EACH MARKED OUT OF 15)

PUPILS' NAMES	1	2	3	4	5	6	7	8	9	10	11	12	13	14	15	16	17	18	19	20	21	22	23	24	25	26	27	28	29	30

Pupil record sheet

READING COMPREHENSION
NAME: CLASS: YEAR:

UNIT	LITERAL	DEDUCTIVE	INFERENTIAL	EVAL.	COMMENTS	MARK	DATE
1	2 3 5 6		1 4 7				
2	3 4	1 2 6 7 9 10	5 8				
3	4 5	8 10	1 2 3 6 7 9				
4	9	4 7	1 2 5 6 8	3 10			
5	2 3	7	1 4 5 6				
6	3 4 10	7 8	1				
7	2 4 8	6 7	1 3 5				
8	4 8	3 7 9 10	1 2 5 6				
9	1 2 3 4 5 7 8	6 9 10					
10		2 3 7	1	4 5 6			
11	5 7	2 3 9 10	1 4 6	8			
12	8	1 3 6 9	2 4 5 6 7 9				
13	2 10 13 14		1 4 6 9 11 15				
14	3 5 8 9 10		4 6 7	1 2			
15	5 7 9	2 4 6 10	1 3 8				
16	3 4 7	9 10	1 2 5 6	8			
17	1 2 8 10 14	3 15	5 7 9				
18	3 4 5 6		1	2 7 8			
19		2 3 4 5	1 6	7			
20	2 3 5 6 7 9 11 12 13 14						
21	4 5	2	1 3 6 7 8 10	9			
22	5	4 7 8	1 2 3 6				
23		3 4 5 6 8 9 11 12	1 2 7 10				
24		3 6 7 8	1 2 4	5			
25	1 3 4 8	5 10	2 6 7	9			
26	1 2 3 4 5 7 8	9 10		6			
27	1 5 6 7 8 9 10		2 4	3			
28	2 3 5 7 8 9 10	6	1 4				
29	1 2 3 4 10 11 12	5 6 7 8 9	13 14	15			
30	4 6 8	2 5 7	1 3 9	10			

PART TWO

Answers, mark scheme and extension activities

Answers follow for each Unit of Key Comprehension Book 3, together with a suggested mark scheme and suggestions for extension activities. Teachers may wish to photocopy relevant pages to allow pupils to mark their own work from the answers provided and to work on the Extension Activities suggested.

Answers

The activities often remind pupils to answer in full sentences in order to develop good practice from the outset. The answers suggested in the Teachers' Handbook are therefore supplied in full sentences where appropriate. In some places, open-ended questions invite a variety of possible answers and where this is the case, guidance is given on the kinds of response that are acceptable.

Mark scheme

The suggested mark scheme marks each Unit out of 15 to allow for some flexibility of response. Teachers may choose to award the suggested marks for accuracy of reading comprehension alone; or they may wish to reserve a part of each allocated mark for spelling, punctuation and sentence construction (for example, whether answers are written in full sentences). A photocopiable whole class record sheet is provided on page 15 and an individual pupil record sheet on page 16.

Extension activities

The extension activities offer opportunities for further work in reading comprehension, language work and writing in a wide range of genres. The specific skills covered are summarised at the end of each set of extension activities.

The disappearing days

GENRE	children's fiction
READING STRATEGIES	skimming; scanning; detailed reading
QUESTION FORM	multiple choice
UNDERSTANDING TESTED	questions 2, 3, 5, 6 - literal; questions 1, 4, 7 - inferential

1   Why did the King of Incrediblania hate washing days?
    c) He didn't like the smell and having washing all over the garden.   (2 marks)

2   Why did the Lord Chancellor hate Mondays?
    b) He had to sign lots of papers on Mondays and wear his official costume.   (2 marks)

3   What does "abolish" mean?
    b) It means to stop something by law.   (2 marks)

4   Which four adjectives did the king use to describe washing days?
    c) uncomfortable, smelly, damp, horrible   (4 marks)

5   What did the Queen do on washing days?
    a) She made sure the washing was hung on the line properly.   (2 marks)

6   How did the Queen feel about abolishing Mondays?
    a) She liked the idea.   (2 marks)

7   Which statement about the King is true?
    b) He has a special dictionary.   (1 mark)

Extension activities

1   If you could abolish one day in the week which day would you abolish?
    Give your reasons.

2   Write about a typical Saturday in your family.

3   Arrange the days of the week in alphabetical order.

    a) What is the first day in the list?
    b) What is the last day in the list?
    c) What is the middle day in the list?

4   Use your class library to find out how the days of the week got their names.
    Write a report on what you find.

5   Use your class library to find out how the months of the year got their names.
    Write a report on what you find.

6   Which is your favourite day of the week? Why?

7   Which is your favourite month of the year? Why?

SPECIFIC SKILLS	expressing a point of view; descriptive writing; research and retrieval; writing an account; language work - alphabetical order

A thoroughly modern Grandmama

GENRE	poem
READING STRATEGIES	skimming; scanning; detailed reading
QUESTION FORM	sentence completion
UNDERSTANDING TESTED	questions 3, 4 - literal; questions 1, 2, 6, 7, 9, 10 - deductive; questions 5, 8 - inferential

1 Picture book grandmothers are usually round and cuddly. How do we know from the poem that this grandmother was probably quite slim?
We know that she was probably quite slim because *the poem says she was always on a diet.* (1.5 marks)

2 Picture book grandmothers have grey hair. How do we know from the poem that this grandmother didn't have grey hair?
We know that she didn't have grey hair because *the poem says she dyes it.* (1.5 marks)

3 Picture book grandmothers are very good at knitting. Did this grandmother knit?
We know that she *didn't knit.* (1.5 marks)

4 What sort of clothes did this grandmother like to wear?
She liked to wear *brightly coloured shirts, jeans and bracelets.* (1.5 marks)

5 How do we know that the girl liked her grandmother being different from picture book grandmothers?
We know because she says she wouldn't *swap her.* (1.5 marks)

6 What does "zooms" (in verse 6) tell you about the way this grandmother drove?
"Zooms" tells me that she drove *very fast.* (1.5 marks)

7 Why does the girl's grandmother have to use a diary to arrange their meetings?
She had to use a diary because *she was so busy and had so many engagements.* (1.5 marks)

8 The girl describes her grandmother as "a complete disaster / as ordinary grannies go". What does she mean by this?
The girl means that *her grandmother is nothing like the traditional / ordinary idea of a grandmother.* (1.5 marks)

9 Which word rhymes with "do" in Verse 4?
The word that rhymes with "do" is *"clue".* (1.5 marks)

10 Which word rhymes with "there" in verse 5?
The word that rhymes with "there" is *"hair".* (1.5 marks)

Extension activities

1 Find a picture of a grandmother in a book in your class library. Make a list of all the ways in which she is like the picture book grandmothers described in the poem.

2 Which sort of grandmothers do you prefer, the thoroughly modern sort or the picture book sort? Why?

3 This grandmother is called "grandmama". Make a list of all the names for grandmothers that the pupils in your class use. Keep a tally and draw up a table of your findings. You may find the following names (and lots of others): grandmother, grandmama, grandma, granny, gran, nan, nana, nannie

SPECIFIC SKILLS	research and retrieval; expressing an opinion; recording findings from a survey

UNIT 3

Insects, colour and camouflage

GENRE	information text
READING STRATEGIES	skimming; scanning; detailed reading
QUESTION FORM	questions requiring answers in complete sentences; true/false
UNDERSTANDING TESTED	questions 4, 5 - literal; questions 8, 10 - deductive; questions 1, 2, 3, 6, 7, 9 - inferential

1 What colour combinations tell birds that an insect would taste terrible if they ate it?
The combinations of red and black or yellow and black tell birds that an insect would taste terrible. *(1 mark)*

2 Explain how some butterflies can scare birds away just by using their wings.
They have markings on their wings like eyes. When they show their wings, birds are frightened because the markings look like cats' eyes (or the eyes of other enemies). *(2 marks)*

3 Why is it very difficult to see grasshoppers when they are among plants and twigs?
It is difficult to see them because they are the same colours as the plants and twigs. *(1 mark)*

4 Why are stick insects very hard to see when they are on twigs?
They are difficult to see because they hold themselves still and look like twigs. They even sway in the breeze to look like the twigs swaying. *(2 marks)*

5 What do the eggs of stick insects look like?
Their eggs look like seeds. *(1 mark)*

6 Is it true that grasshoppers can fly?
Yes, it is true that grasshoppers can fly. *(1 mark)*

7 Is it true that birds eat caterpillars?
Yes, it is true that birds eat caterpillars when possible. *(1 mark)*

8 Read the "Flash colours" section again. Which word in the section means "bewildered"?
The word that means "bewildered" is "confused". *(2 marks)*

9 Explain what "camouflage" means.
"Camouflage" means the colouring of a creature makes it difficult to see because it looks like its surroundings. *(2 marks)*

10 Explain what "slender" means.
"Slender" means slim or thin. *(2 marks)*

Extension activities

1 Harmless insects are said to mimic the warning colours of wasps and bees. What does "mimic" mean?

2 What are the three ways in which the pussmoth protects itself?

3 What are predators?

4 Peppered moths have one form of camouflage for the country and one form for the town.How are the two forms different and why are two forms necessary?

5 Another fascinating creature who is master of the art of camouflage is the chameleon. Use books in your class library to find out all you can about how the chameleon protects itself from enemies.

SPECIFIC SKILLS	additional comprehension questions; research and retrieval; writing an account of findings

The air raid

GENRE	children's fiction
READING STRATEGIES	skimming; scanning; detailed reading
QUESTION FORM	multiple choice
UNDERSTANDING TESTED	question 9 - literal; questions 4, 7 - deductive; questions 1, 2, 5, 6, 8 - inferential; questions 3, 10 - evaluative

1 Where was Harry when the bomb fell?
   c) *Harry was in the shelter in the garden.* *(1.5 marks)*

2 Why did the warden want to know the names of Harry's mother and father?
   a) *He wanted the names for official records.* *(1.5 marks)*

3 Why didn't the warden answer when Harry said, "Where's our house?"
   c) *He didn't want to tell Harry that his house had been blown up by a bomb.* *(1.5 marks)*

4 If a gas pipe is "fractured", what has happened to it?
   c) *It has been broken.* *(1.5 marks)*

5 Why did Harry run up the garden path?
   a) *He wanted to find his parents.* *(1.5 marks)*

6 What was the number of Harry's house?
   c) *His house was number 9.* *(1.5 marks)*

7 Why did the warden want to get Harry to the Rest Centre as quickly as possible?
   b) *He wanted to get Hary away from the bomb site and thought Harry would need help and support after what had happened.* *(1.5 marks)*

8 Why were the Humphrey family so pale?
   a) *They were in a state of shock.* *(1.5 marks)*

9 Where were the Simpson family when the bomb fell?
   c) *They were in their garden.* *(1.5 marks)*

10 Which sentence best describes Harry's feelings at the end of the passage?
   b) *He felt frightened and unhappy.* *(1.5 marks)*

Extension activities

1 Basing your answer on the passage, make a list of the duties of a warden after an air raid has taken place.

2 How can you tell from the passage that Harry is in a state of shock?

3 What words first show us that the warden knows Harry's parents are dead?

4 Choose three adjectives from the following list that you think describe the warden best. Explain why you think so.

   firm   **gentle**   **observant**
   rough   **rude**   **tactful**

5 Pretend you are the warden. Write your diary for the day described in the passage.

SPECIFIC SKILLS	additional comprehension questions; writing in character; writing a diary

GENRE	poem
READING STRATEGIES	skimming; scanning; detailed reading
QUESTION FORM	questions requiring answers in complete sentences
UNDERSTANDING TESTED	questions 2, 3 - literal; question 7 - deductive; questions 1, 4, 5, 6 - inferential

1 To whom was the boy speaking when he said, "Remember me?"
He was speaking to the boy who bullied him in the past. (1 mark)

2 List all the ways in which the boy had been made to feel hurt and rejected four years before.
He was rejected as a possible friend.
He wasn't allowed to join in games.
He wasn't invited to the party.
He was physically bullied.
He was mentally bullied. (2.5 marks)

3 In what ways is he different now?
He doesn't cry so easily. He is a foot taller, and bigger and stronger. He is
popular and he is more grown-up now. (1.5 marks)

4 Why did the boy not take his revenge when he had the chance?
He was tempted to take his revenge but he didn't because he remembered how
it felt to be the victim. (2 marks)

5 What did he do instead of taking revenge?
He offered his hand in forgiveness and friendship. (2 marks)

6 Why did he "feel much stronger" when he decided not to take revenge?
He felt stronger because he knew it took more courage to make friends than to
make enemies. (2 marks)

7 What does "sought" mean?
"Sought" means "looked for". (1 mark)

8 What does "too" mean?
"Too" means "also". (1 mark)

9 What does "punchbag" mean?
"Punchbag" means "a stuffed bag used for practice in boxing". (1 mark)

10 What does "popular" mean?
"Popular" means "liked by many people". (1 mark)

Extension activities

1 What advice would you give any child who is being bullied?

2 The headteacher of your school has decided to try to stop bullying in school
and makes an announcement to all the pupils one Monday morning. Write down
what the announcement says.

3 Write a short story in which a bully is made to feel ashamed.

SPECIFIC SKILLS	reflective writing; giving advice; writing a speech in character; writing a story

U N I T
6

Earthquakes

GENRE	information text and tables
READING STRATEGIES	skimming; scanning; detailed reading
QUESTION FORM	true / false
UNDERSTANDING TESTED	questions 3, 4, 10 - literal; questions 7, 8 - deductive; question 1 - inferential

The true statements are:

1 *California is a high-risk area for earthquakes.* *(2.5 marks)*

3 *Earthquakes are caused by huge plates of rock moving in the Earth's crust.* *(2.5 marks)*

4 *A major earthquake takes place every few months.* *(2.5 marks)*

7 *A major earthquake registers 7 on the Richter scale.* *(2.5 marks)*

8 *During major earthquakes, buildings are destroyed.* *(2.5 marks)*

10 *The modified Mercalli scale measures how much the ground shakes.* *(2.5 marks)*

Extension activities

1 Explain the basic differences between the Richter Scale and the Modified Mercalli Scale.

2 Describe the effects of a major earthquake on a large town.

3 Explain why some earthquakes need not cause concern.

4 What do the following words mean?

a) tremors
b) collapse
c) liable
d) predict

5 **Seismology** is the study of earthquakes. Complete these other -ologies.

a) **sp _ _ _ ology**: study of caves

b) **as _ _ ology**: study of effects of stars on our lives

c) **b _ ology**: study of plants and animals

d) **camp _ _ ology**: study of bells and bell-ringing

e) **g _ ology**: study of earth's crust

f) **ps _ _ _ ology**: study of human mind

g) **ar _ _ _ology**: study of ancient buildings

h) **tox _ _ ology**: study of poisons

i) **so _ _ ology**: study of society and social groups

j) **tec _ _ ology**: study of practical uses of scientific discoveries

SPECIFIC SKILLS	additional comprehension questions; vocabulary

The runt

GENRE	children's fiction
READING STRATEGIES	skimming; scanning; detailed reading
QUESTION FORM	questions requiring answers in complete sentences
UNDERSTANDING TESTED	questions 2, 4, 8 - literal; questions 6, 7 - deductive; questions 1, 3, 5 - inferential

1 What was Fern's surname?
  Fern's surname was Arable. (1 mark)

2 How old was Fern?
  Fern was eight years old. (1 mark)

3 What was Mr Arable going to do with the axe?
  He was going to use it to kill the weak little pig (the runt) because they always
  cause trouble. (2 marks)

4 What did he decide to give Fern to look after?
  He decided to give the little pig to Fern to look after. (1 mark)

5 What do you find out about what Mr Arable's personality is like from this passage?
  Include all the details you can find.
  He loves his daughter, Fern, very much. He is a very practical man and is not sentimental.
  He understands how she feels about the little runt being killed. He is kind to Fern and
  explains his actions to her. He and his wife understand each other.
  He has a sense of humour. He indulges Fern. (4 marks)

6 What do the following words mean?
  a) A hoghouse is a pigsty.
  b) Sneakers are trainers.
  c) A pitcher is a jug. (3 marks)

7 Which word in the passage means "the smallest, weakest pig in a litter"?
  The word "runt" means "the smallest, weakest pig in the litter". (1 mark)

8 What did the kitchen smell of a breakfast time?
  The kitchen smelled of coffee, bacon, damp plaster and wood-smoke. (2 marks)

Extension activities

1 Imagine you are Fern. Write an account of the exciting morning when you
  were given a little pig to look after.

2 Write the conversation between Mr and Mrs Arable after Fern has gone to school
  and the little pig is asleep in his carton.

3 Why do you think Mr Arable decides to give Fern the pig to raise?
  Write a list of all the possible reasons he might have.

4 Have you ever had a pet?
  Make a list of all the ways in which it is hard work to keep a pet.
  Make another list of all the ways in which it is fun to keep a pet.

SPECIFIC SKILLS	writing in character; writing a conversation; writing a list; reflective writing

A Martian comes to stay

GENRE	children's fiction
READING STRATEGIES	skimming; scanning; detailed reading
QUESTION FORM	questions requiring answers in complete sentences
UNDERSTANDING TESTED	questions 4, 8 - literal; questions 3, 7, 9, 10 - deductive; questions 1, 2, 5, 6 - inferential

1 How did Peter react when he opened the door and found a Martian there?
   He was calm and treated the Martian like any other visitor.   (1.5 marks)

2 What was Gran doing when the Martian knocked at the door?
   She was knitting.   (1.5 marks)

3 What is an emergency landing?
   *An emergency landing is when something is wrong in the aircraft and the pilot has to
   change the plan and come down unexpectedly.*   (1.5 marks)

4 Why didn't the Martians have their own toolbox in the spaceship?
   It was left behind on Mars.   (1.5 marks)

5 The Martian "padded away up the lane". What does "padded" mean?
   "Padded" means that he walked softly.   (1.5 marks)

6 Why was Gran's reaction so unusual when Peter told her there was a Martian at the door?
   *Most grandmothers would have thought that Peter was being silly and making it up,
   but Gran reacted as though it was a normal everyday thing to happen.*   (1.5 marks)

7 Gran's cottage was isolated. What does "isolated" mean?
   "Isolated" means it was a long way from any other house.   (1.5 marks)

8 Why did Gran wish that she had offered the Martian a cup of tea?
   She thought he would be thirsty because he had come all the way from Mars.   (1.5 marks)

9 Which word means a woman whose husband is dead?
   "Widow" means a woman whose husband is dead.   (1.5 marks)

10 Why was the Martian agitated when he came back?
   He was upset because the spaceship had gone without him.   (1.5 marks)

Extension activities

1 Draw a picture of what you think the Martian's spaceship looks like.

   Write a description of all the gadgets the spaceship has, inside and out.

2 Write a letter from Peter to his parents, telling them what has happened so far
   at Gran's.

3 Sometimes we run two words together to make one shorter word.

   For example we say <u>can't</u> instead of <u>can not</u>.
   These shortened words are called contractions.

   Make a list of all the contractions that are used in this story.
   Then write out the words that they stand for in full.

SPECIFIC SKILLS	imaginative writing; descriptive writing; writing a letter in character; contractions

Ladislao Biro

GENRE	information text
READING STRATEGIES	skimming; scanning; detailed reading
QUESTION FORM	questions requiring answers in complete sentences; true/false
UNDERSTANDING TESTED	questions 1, 2, 3, 4, 5, 7, 8 - literal; questions 6, 9, 10 - deductive

1 Where was Ladislao Biro born?
He was born in Hungary. *(1 mark)*

2 How did working as a magazine editor help him to invent the biro?
*He saw quick-drying inks used for printing magazines and this gave him the idea of
using these inks in pens.* *(1 mark)*

3 Why did he sell his invention in 1944?
*He sold his invention because he hadn't got the money to manufacture and market
it on a large scale himself.* *(2 marks)*

4 Which French firm still manufactures his invention?
The French firm Bic still produces the pen he invented. *(2 marks)*

5 Find four reasons in the passage for the popularity of ballpoint pens.
*Accept any four from: ballpoint pens don't leak; the ink is quick-drying/doesn't
smudge/doesn't need blotting; the pens are cheap; they are easy to carry; they are
disposable; they don't have to be refilled.* *(2 marks)*

6 Is it true that Ladislao Biro made a huge fortune out of his invention?
No, it is false. *(1 mark)*

7 In what year did Ladislao Biro leave Hungary?
He left Hungary in 1939. *(1 mark)*

8 What happened to Biro's invention in 1943?
It began to be manufactured in 1943. *(1 mark)*

9 "Biro sank into obscurity in South America". Explain in your own words what this means.
It means that Biro lived a quiet, private life in South America so no one knew where he was. *(2 marks)*

10 "His name has become a household word." Explain in your own words what this means.
*This means that his name, "Biro", has become a word that everyone knows and uses
because he gave his name to his invention and now ballpoint pens are also called biros.* *(2 marks)*

Extension activities

1 List the advantages and disadvantages of fountain pens and ballpoint pens.

2 Find out the full names of the people who gave their names to the following discoveries
and inventions.

a) Braille	e) sandwich
b) cardigan	f) Bunsen burner
c) diesel	g) Morse code
d) Hoover	h) wellington boots

SPECIFIC SKILLS	reflective writing; writing a list; vocabulary: eponyms; research and retrieval

The woman, the boy and the lion

GENRE	folk tale
READING STRATEGIES	skimming; scanning; detailed reading
QUESTION FORM	questions requiring answers in complete sentences
UNDERSTANDING TESTED	questions 2, 3, 7 - deductive; question 1 - inferential; question 4, 5, 6, - evaluative

1 What did Fanaye do to try to make the little boy like her?
Fanaye cooked specially nice food for him, she tried to kiss him, she tried to cuddle him and she tried to tell him stories. (2 marks)

2 Why do you think the little boy was so unfriendly at first?
Accept any sensible answers. Answers might suggest some of the following:
He wanted his real mother; he didn't want to share his father with anyone else; he didn't know her very well and was shy or frightened; he had heard stories about cruel stepmothers and was frightened. (2 marks)

3 What is another word for "moral"?
Another word for "moral" is "lesson". (1 mark)

4 Why did the wise man make Fanaye bring him the hair from the lion's tail when he could have told her right away that she would just have to be very patient?
He wanted to prove his point by letting Fanaye find out the truth of it for herself. (1 mark)

5 In what ways was the boy like the wild black-maned lion?
The boy was fierce and unfriendly. He wouldn't let Fanaye touch him. He escaped to his bedroom (like a den) to get away from her. He didn't trust her. He would not make friends quickly and needed a lot of patience from Fanaye. (1 mark)

6 What do you find out about what Fanaye's personality is like from this story?
Include all the details you can find.
Accept any of the following:
She wants to be a good mother to the little boy. She is patient. She does her best to make friends. She isn't afraid to admit failure or ask for advice. She fulfils the wise man's conditions and doesn't try to cheat. She is brave and overcomes her great fear and risks her life. She thinks of others and isn't selfish. She is gentle. (2 marks)

7 What other words could be used instead without changing the meaning?
a) tales - *stories*
b) down-hearted - *depressed / despondent*
c) peaceably - *calmly* (2 marks)
d) contendedly - *happily*
e) manage - *achieve*
f) trusted - *felt safe with / had confidence in* (6 marks)

Extension activities

1 Has there ever been an occasion when your patience was your patience rewarded? Write about it.

2 Write a story of your own that illustrates the following moral:
If you want to have a friend, you must be a friend.

SPECIFIC SKILLS	personal writing; writing a story with a moral

Tom

UNIT 11

GENRE	children's fiction
READING STRATEGIES	skimming; scanning; detailed reading
QUESTION FORM	questions requiring answers in complete sentences
UNDERSTANDING TESTED	questions 5, 7 - literal; questions 1, 4, 6 - inferential; questions 2, 3, 9, 10 - deductive; question 8 - evaluative

1 What were the two reasons why Tom could not sleep?
Tom could not sleep because he had indigestion from his aunt's rich cooking. He also hadn't had any exercise. (2 marks)

2 What is the difference between sleeping and dozing?
When you sleep you sleep deeply for a long time. When you doze you are only half asleep and you keep waking up. (2 marks)

3 Why was Uncle Alan so cross when he found Tom still reading in bed late at night?
He was cross because he thought that Tom needed his sleep. (2 marks)

4 How did Tom feel about not being allowed to read in bed for more than ten minutes?
He didn't mind about not reading but time dragged even more in the dark. (2 marks)

5 How did Tom spend his days at Aunt Gwen's?
Tom had to stay indoors all the time. He did crosswords and jigsaw puzzles and sometimes helped Aunt Gwen to cook. He was bored. (2 marks)

6 Why wasn't he allowed to go outdoors and meet people?
Tom had to stay away from people in case they caught measles from him. (1 mark)

7 Which sound did Tom get used to hearing during the night?
Tom got used to hearing the striking of the grandfather clock. (1 mark)

8 Which word best describes how Tom felt at Aunt Gwen's?
"Bored" best describes how Tom felt. (1 mark)

9 What does "monologue" mean?
A monologue is when just one person is talking. (1 mark)

10 What does "persevere" mean?
"Persevere" means to keep on trying. (1 mark)

Extension activities

1 What do the following words mean?
   a) monotone
   b) monorail
   c) monoplane
   d) monopoly

2 How could Tom explain to his aunt and uncle why he can't sleep at night and why he is so bored during the day? Write down what he could say. Take care not to hurt the feelings of the aunt and uncle. They are both very kind but they don't know much about looking after children.

3 Describe a time when you were ill.

SPECIFIC SKILLS	dictionary work; vocabulary: mono- words; writing in character; personal writing

Lucy's dream

GENRE	children's fiction
READING STRATEGIES	skimming; scanning; detailed reading
QUESTION FORM	questions requiring answers in complete sentences
UNDERSTANDING TESTED	question 8 - literal; questions 1, 3, 6, 9 - deductive; questions 2, 4, 5, 6, 7, 9 - inferential

1 In what part of a house is the attic?
The attic is at the very top of the house, just under the roof. (1 mark)

2 What sounds could be heard in Lucy's bedroom?
There were the sounds of a lark singing and Lucy making noises in her sleep. (2 marks)

3 Explain clearly what a nightmare is.
A nightmare is an unpleasant and frightening dream. (1 mark)

4 What sounds did Lucy hear in her nightmare?
Lucy heard the noise of the stairs as someone walked up them, the rattling of the latch and the girl's voice. (3 marks)

5 Why would Lucy have needed binoculars to see the lark?
She would have needed binoculars to see it because it was so far away.

6 What sound do you make if you whimper?
You make little half-crying noises. (1 mark)

7 What was it that stopped Lucy whimpering?
Lucy stopped whimpering when she heard the sound of the door opening in her dream. (1 mark)

8 What made the girl in Lucy's nightmare look so dreadful?
The girl looked dreadful because she was covered in slimy, black oil. (1 mark)

9 Find the following words in the passage. What other words could be used instead without changing the meaning?
a) pitch - *very / completely*
b) mingled - *mixed / blended*
c) peculiar - *strange / unusual / odd* (3 marks)

10 Finish the last sentence in your own words to show what Lucy was thinking.
But if the door was now open, *then the nightmare was not a dream but had really happened.* (2 marks)

Extension activities

1 What is it in the first paragraph that is making the lark's body seem to flicker?

2 Why is the lark's song described as a strange sound?

3 Do you find Lucy's nightmare frightening? What is the most frightening part? Why?

4 Plurals of words ending in -f and -fe. Write the plurals of the following words.

a) roof	e) loaf
b) handkerchief	f) sheriff
c) knife	g) shelf
d) giraffe	h) cuff

SPECIFIC SKILLS	additional comprehension questions; plurals of -f and -fe words

Swans with names

GENRE	information text
READING STRATEGIES	skimming; scanning; detailed reading
QUESTION FORM	true / false
UNDERSTANDING TESTED	questions 2, 10, 13, 14 - literal; questions 1, 4, 6, 9, 11, 15 - inferential

The true statements are:

1 *Bewick's swans stay with the same partner all their life.* (1.5 marks)

2 *Bewick's swans can live for more than twenty-five years.* (1.5 marks)

4 *Peter Scott discovered that no two Bewick's swans look exactly alike.* (1.5 marks)

6 *It is a crime to injure a swan.* (1.5 marks)

9 *Bewick's swan eggs hatch out in Siberia.* (1.5 marks)

10 *No two Bewick's swans have the same pattern on their beaks.* (1.5 marks)

11 *Some swans in North America fly away to spend the winter in a different place.* (1.5 marks)

13 *Bewick's swans stay with their parents for their first winter.* (1.5 marks)

14 *Peter Scott knew the Bewick's swans at Slimbridge well enough to give them names.* (1.5 marks)

15 *Bewick's swans spend every summer in Siberia.* (1.5 marks)

Extension activities

1 What is an estuary?

2 What does "migrate" mean?

3 Which word in the passage means "beaks"?

4 Why is it so important to protect the marshes and estuaries used by swans as resting-places on their journeys?

5 Describe the migration timetable of the Bewick's swans.

6 Where is Siberia?

7 a) What do we call an adult male swan?   c _ _

   b) What do we call an adult female swan?   p _ _

   c) What do we call a young swan?   c _ _ _ _ _

8 What is meant by a person's swan-song?

9 Use books from your class library to help you to draw a map showing the route that the swans go take every year.

   Add a scale to the map and work out approximately how far the swans fly on their journey.

SPECIFIC SKILLS	additional comprehension questions; dictionary work; research and retrieval; plotting a route on a map

GENRE	information text presented as narrative (faction)
READING STRATEGIES	skimming; scanning; detailed reading
QUESTION FORM	multiple choice
UNDERSTANDING TESTED	questions 3, 5, 8, 9, 10 - literal; questions 4, 6, 7 - inferential; questions 1, 2 - evaluative

1 What was Florence Nightingale's reaction to what she saw?
   b) She was horrified and angry. (1.5 marks)

2 What did the doctors think about Florence Nightingale coming to work at the hospital?
   a) They thought she was going to be a nuisance. (1.5 marks)

3 Why did operations take place in the wards in front of all the other patients?
   b) There was nowhere else to go. (1.5 marks)

4 What kind of hospital was this one?
   c) It was a hospital for the Army. (1.5 marks)

5 Why was the hospital so badly equipped?
   b) The Army wouldn't give any money to buy equipment. (1.5 marks)

6 Why were the patients still wearing their filthy uniforms?
   c) There were no clean clothes for them to wear. (1.5 marks)

7 Which set of adjectives best describes conditions in the hospital?
   c) overcrowded, dirty and cold. (1.5 marks)

8 Florence Nightingale had £30,000 to spend on whatever was necessary.
   Where did the money come from?
   c) It came from the general public in England. (1.5 marks)

9 What did Florence Nightingale decide to buy first?
   c) scrubbing brushes (1.5 marks)

10 Why did Florence Nightingale come to the hospital?
   a) She came to be in charge of all the nursing care. (1.5 marks)

Extension activities

1 Write a description of Florence Nightingale using the evidence in the passage.

2 Make a list of all the shortages that made life at the hospital so uncomfortable.

3 Florence Nightingale's voice at one point "beat about the doctors like a whip". What does this tell you about the way her voice sounded?

4 Why do you think Florence Nightingale didn't tell the officers how much money she had?

5 Use your class library to find out why Florence Nightingale was called the "lady with a lamp" by patients at the Crimean hospital.

6 Imagine that you are one of the men lying in dirty clothes on the floor of one of the biggest wards. Write a letter home telling your wife about the arrival of Florence Nightingale and how everything began to get better once she came.

SPECIFIC SKILLS	additional questions; making a list; research and retrieval; writing up findings; empathetic writing; writing a letter

Sumitra's story

GENRE	children's fiction
READING STRATEGIES	skimming; scanning; detailed reading
QUESTION FORM	questions requiring answers in complete sentences
UNDERSTANDING TESTED	questions 5, 7, 9 - literal; questions 2, 4, 6, 10 - deductive; questions 1, 3, 8 - inferential

1 Why was Mr Patel buying fireworks?
They were for a display at his sister's wedding. *(1 mark)*

2 What does "poring over catalogues" mean?
It means looking at the catalogues closely and attentively. *(1 mark)*

3 What did Sumitra call her father?
She called him Bap. *(1 mark)*

4 Which word in the passage means "sleepily"?
"Drowsily" means "sleepily". *(1 mark)*

5 Which of the following items was not a firework in Mr Patel's catalogue?
Coral Cascade was not in the catalogue. *(1 mark)*

6 What does "a well-thumbed brochure" mean?
It means a catalogue that has been read again and again and is getting tatty because it has been handled so much. *(2 marks)*

7 What relation was Mr Patel to Leela?
He was her brother. *(1 mark)*

8 What did Mr Patel mean when he said, "Pacing is important"?
He meant that it was important to set off the fireworks at just the right moment to get the best effect. *(2 marks)*

9 What do you find out about the place where this passage is set? Describe the place in your own words.
The passage is set in the countryside in a place where it is hot, dry and dusty. It is very sunny and there are a few villages and small towns. There are hills with waterfalls and lakes at the bottom. *(3 marks)*

10 Mr Patel was "something of an expert" at arranging firework displays. What does this mean?
This means that he was very good at arranging firework displays. *(2 marks)*

Extension activities

1 Explain in your own words what Mr Patel's idea of a good firework display was.

2 What is another word for "brochure"?

3 When the same letters are repeated close together, this is called alliteration.
For example, "Peter Piper picked a peck of pickled peppers".
a) Write down the names of the fireworks which are alliterative.
b) Make up four more alliterative names for fireworks.
c) Make up some alliterative nicknames for yourself.

SPECIFIC SKILLS	additional questions requiring evaluative responses; alliteration

UNIT 16 Black Beauty

GENRE	children's classic fiction
READING STRATEGIES	skimming; scanning; detailed reading
QUESTION FORM	questions requiring answers in complete sentences
UNDERSTANDING TESTED	questions 3, 4, 7 - literal; questions 9, 10 - deductive; questions 1, 2, 5, 6 - inferential; question 8 - evaluative

1 How can you tell from the way he fitted Black Beauty with a bridle and saddle that the coachman was a kind man?
You can tell he was kind because he took care to see that the bridle was buckled comfortably and he made sure that the saddle was the right size for Black Beauty's back. (2 marks)

2 The coachman praised Black Beauty for four of the reasons below.
Write down the correct four reasons.
a) He can gallop well. c) He is obedient. d) He is brave. e) He has been well trained. (2 marks)

3 Write down everything you learn about Black Beauty's appearance.
The horse was black. He had a soft bright coat and a broad back. He was very handsome. His face was sweet and good-tempered. His eyes were fine and intelligent. (2 marks)

4 What did Black Beauty think of his new owner, Squire Gordon?
Black Beauty thought he was a very good and considerate rider. (1 mark)

5 How can you tell that John Manly, the coachman, was one of Squire Gordon's servants?
John Manly calls Squire Gordon "sir" whereas the Squire calls him by his first name. He is polite and respectful when he is given orders. He is clear and business-like when answering questions and doesn't disagree or presume. (2 marks)

6 Who is the narrator (the one telling the story) in this passage?
The narrator is the horse, Black Beauty. (1 mark)

7 What were the three names Mrs. Gordon suggested for her husband's new horse?
She suggested Ebony, Blackbird and Black Beauty. (1 mark)

8 Which one of the three names would you have chosen? Why?
Reward any sensibly justified choice. (2 marks)

9 What does "ill-used" mean?
"Ill-used" means "treated badly". (1 mark)

10 What does "counsel" mean?
"Counsel" means "advice". (1 mark)

Extension activities

1 Use dictionaries and reference books to find out what jobs the following people do.

a) coachman   f) colt-breaker

b) ostler   g) blacksmith

c) carter   h) plough boy

d) groom   i) stable boy

e) farrier   j) horse doctor

SPECIFIC SKILLS	vocabulary of occupations to do with horses

The cloth of emperors

GENRE	information text
READING STRATEGIES	skimming; scanning; detailed reading
QUESTION FORM	true/false
UNDERSTANDING TESTED	questions 1, 2, 8, 10, 14 - literal; questions 3, 15 - deductive; questions 5, 7, 9 - inferential

The true sentences are:

1 *The silkworm is not a worm.* (1.5 marks)

2 *The silk is liquid when it first comes out of a silkworm's body.* (1.5 marks)

3 *No water can get into the cocoon.* (1.5 marks)

5 *If human begins are going to use the silk of the cocoon, they must kill the silkworm.* (1.5 marks)

7 *The silkmoth lives for only a few days after she has laid her eggs.* (1.5 marks)

8 *Over one hundred silkworms are needed to produce enough silk to make a tie.* (1.5 marks)

9 *Silk is made in some European countries today.* (1.5 marks)

10 *It takes 630 cocoons of silk to make a blouse.* (1.5 marks)

14 *Silkworms don't like strong smells.* (1.5 marks)

15 *It is not very quick or easy to make silk.* (1.5 marks)

Extension activities

1 What do the following words mean?
   a) tapestries
   b) disclosed
   c) harmony
   d) garments
   e) emperor

2 Find the words in the passage that match these definitions:
   a) suffocated   s _ _ _ _ _ _
   b) long Japanese robe with wide sleeves   k _ _ _ _ _
   c) rearing silkworms to make silk   s _ _ _ _ _ _ _ _ _
   d) followed or obeyed rules   o _ _ _ _ _ _ _

3 Explain how the title is relevant to the passage.

4 Using the information in the passage, write a paragraph about the life cycle of the silkmoth.

5 Now you have read about the way silkworms are reared and silk is produced, do you think the silkworms are well looked after? Explain your answer.

6 Imagine that you work as a "silkworm mother". Describe a typical day at work. How do you dress? What are your duties? What do you enjoy about your job? What don't you enjoy?

SPECIFIC SKILLS	vocabulary questions; chronological writing; expressing an opinion; writing in character; descriptive writing

The bully asleep

GENRE	poem
READING STRATEGIES	skimming; scanning; detailed reading
QUESTION FORM	questions requiring answers in complete sentences
UNDERSTANDING TESTED	questions 3, 4, 5, 6 - literal; question 1 - inferential; questions 2, 7, 8 - evaluative

1 What was the name of the bully who was asleep?
His name was Bill Craddock. *(1 mark)*

2 What does the word "timidly" (verse 2) tell us about how the children felt when they lifted up his head and let it sink back on the desk again?
"Timidly" tells us that the children felt shy and nervous about touching the bully in case he woke up and was violent. *(2 marks)*

3 Why was the bully so tired?
He was tired because he never got a good night's sleep. His mother never made sure he went to bed. *(2 marks)*

4 What did Jimmy do to get his own back on the bully?
Jimmy took Bill's pen away and hid it. *(2 marks)*

5 Why did the boys think it would be a good opportunity to kick him hard even though it would wake him up?
They thought it would be a good idea because he wouldn't know who was responsible. They would have the satisfaction of revenge without having to suffer for it. *(2 marks)*

6 Write down four acts of revenge that they discuss and plan but don't actually carry out before the end of the poem.
They discussed kicking him, filling his pockets with rubbish, sticking pins into him and putting ink down his neck. *(2 marks)*

7 Why was Jane "wide-eyed" at the boys' talk?
She could not believe that anyone could think of such horrible things to do. She was astonished and horrified. *(2 marks)*

8 Why do you think Jane wanted to comfort Bill Craddock?
She felt sorry for him because she suddenly saw how pathetic, isolated and unloved he was. *(2 marks)*

Extension activities

1 What was Miss Andrew's reaction to the boy falling asleep in her lesson?

2 Jimmy sounds sympathetic to the bully in verse three, but how can you tell later in the poem that he wanted his revenge?

3 Are Jimmy and Roger being bullies too?

4 Why do you think the poet has chosen to write about the bully asleep rather than the bully awa

5 Write about the incident from the point of view of Jimmy, Roger or Jane. Explain how you felt.

6 Write a continuation, either as a poem, story or scene from a play, called "The Bully Awakes".

7 Write a letter to your headteacher giving advice on how you think bullying should be dealt with in your school.

8 "You should really feel sorry for a bully." Do you agree or disagree with this point of view? Wh

SPECIFIC SKILLS	additional comprehension questions; empathetic writing; extending the story; writing a letter; giving advice; expressing and justifying an opinion

The chicken gave it to me

GENRE	children's fiction
READING STRATEGIES	skimming; scanning; detailed reading
QUESTION FORM	questions requiring answers in complete sentences
UNDERSTANDING TESTED	questions 2, 3, 4, 5- deductive; questions 1, 6 - inferential; question 7 - evaluative

1   What made the book look as if a chicken had made it and written it?
*The book was tiny and made of a bit of pecked farm sack. The edges of the cover
were not cut with scissors but pecked by a beak. The writing was thin and scratchy.*   (2 marks)

2   Explain exactly how Andrew must have been feeling when he repeated helplessly that
a chicken had given the book to him.
*He couldn't see how to convince Gemma. He knew it was impossible to believe and that
he wouldn't believe it either, in her place. He wanted to convince her because she was
his friend and he wanted to share the excitement of the little book with her.
He felt miserable.*   (2 marks)

3   What is the difference between strolling and strutting?
Strolling is walking slowly and casually. Strutting is walking in a stiff-legged, proud way.   (1 mark)

4   Find the following words in the passage. What other words or phrases could be used
instead without changing the meaning?
a) ridiculous - *silly, foolish*
b) ferocious - *fierce, angry, dangerous and violent*
c) ignore - *pay no attention to, take no notice of*   (3 marks)

5   Explain clearly the special meaning of the following words.
a) to repeat - *means to say something for a second time.*
b) to interrupt - *means to break in when somebody else is talking.*
c) to hiss - *means to speak in a loud, urgent whisper.*   (3 marks)

6   Why did Gemma believe Andrew in the end? Explain what was convincing about
the way Andrew told his story.
*Andrew described what happened clearly. He insisted it was true and he didn't change
his story. He was very serious.. He pointed out that it was not something he would
choose to happen to him. He seemed amazed himself at what had happened.*   (2 marks)

7   What do you find out about what Gemma's personality was like from this passage?
*Gemma was sensible and outspoken and said what she thought. She could be a bit bossy
and pointed out mistakes when she spotted them. She was clever with words. Gemma
must have been a good friend and fun to share things with if Andrew is so desperate to
convince her.*   (2 marks)

Extension activities

1   Write a conversation where you are trying to convince someone that you are telling the truth.
(Make it clear whether you succeed or not in the end.)

2   Read the definitions and complete the words. (They are all to do with ways of walking.)
a) to move smoothly and silently: g _ _ _ _
b) to go slowly, wasting time: d _ _ _ _ _
c) to move along on hands and knees: c _ _ _ _
d) to walk with tiny steps, trying to look elegant: mi _ _ _

SPECIFIC SKILLS	writing a conversation; vocabulary - verbs of walking

Treasure hunting

GENRE	information text
READING STRATEGIES	skimming; scanning; detailed reading
QUESTION FORM	true / false
UNDERSTANDING TESTED	all questions - literal

The true sentences are:

2 *There are more undiscovered bottle dumps than secret hoards of buried coins.* *(1.5 marks)*

3 *Some people collect bottles.* *(1.5 marks)*

5 *Toothpaste used to be sold in pots with china lids.* *(1.5 marks)*

6 *You can clean the outside of bottles in a bucket of sand.* *(1.5 marks)*

7 *Bottles can be worth a lot of money.* *(1.5 marks)*

9 *You can use lemon juice to remove some stains.* *(1.5 marks)*

11 *There could be a thousand bottles in some small rubbish dumps.* *(1.5 marks)*

12 *You can damage bottles you dig up if you wash them right away.* *(1.5 marks)*

13 *Some lemonade bottles used to have marbles instead of corks.* *(1.5 marks)*

14 *Country people used to bury their rubbish.* *(1.5 marks)*

Extension activities

1 Why is an undiscovered hundred-year-old rubbish dump likely to have so many bottles and jars in it?

2 Why were rubbish tips dug downwind of houses?

3 Why should glass bottles not be cleaned for at least twenty-four hours after being dug up?

4 List all the ways suggested for cleaning the insides of bottles.

5 "Sand scours the glass clean." What does "scours" mean?

6 The writer makes treasure hunting for bottles, jars and stone lids sound very exciting. Has he succeeded in interesting you? Write about whether the passage makes you feel interested in this hobby and why.

7 If you are a collector of something, write about your collection and try to explain why it is fun being a collector.

8 Write a story about some children who dig up a very rare bottle. What do they do when they discover that they could sell it for a large sum of money?

SPECIFIC SKILLS	additional questions; explaining and justifying a response to an article; personal writing; reflective writing; narrative writing from given data

The Borrowers

GENRE	classic children's fiction
READING STRATEGIES	skimming; scanning; detailed reading
QUESTION FORM	questions requiring answers in complete sentences
UNDERSTANDING TESTED	questions 4, 5 - literal; question 2 - deductive; questions 1, 3, 6, 7, 8, 10 - inferential; question 9 - evaluative

1 How did Kate feel at the beginning of the passage?
   She is puzzled because she couldn't understand how she had lost her needle. (1.5 marks)

2 What is a hassock?
   A hassock is a hard cushion. (1.5 marks)

3 What did Mrs May think had happened to all the needles that Kate's mother had lost?
   She thought the Borrowers had probably taken them. (1.5 marks)

4 What made Kate believe that the Borrowers must exist?
   She knew that lots of small objects regularly disappeared and Mrs May's story seemed to explain this. (1.5 marks)

5 Where did Mrs May live when she was a little girl?
   She lived in India. (1.5 marks)

6 How did Mrs May's brother die?
   He died in battle. (1.5 marks)

7 Did Mrs May think her brother had been telling the truth about the Borrowers?
   She was almost sure that he had been telling the truth. (1.5 marks)

8 Why might her brother have made up the stories?
   He might have made them up to impress his sisters and to make up for being younger. (1.5 marks)

9 How did Mrs May feel when she talked about her brother?
   She was amused by his stories and also seems sad when she thinks about him now. (1.5 marks)

10 Why didn't Kate want the lamp to be lit?
   She wanted Mrs May to finish the story instead. (1.5 marks)

Extension activities

1 What details show that this story is set in the past? List the references that seem old-fashioned.

2 What did Mrs May mean when she says that her brother died "a hero's death"?

3 Mrs May's brother stayed with his great-aunt when he was convalescing from rheumatic fever. If the lady is his great-aunt, whose aunt would she be?

4 The Borrowers are little people who make good use of small everyday objects that they borrow. Choose three of the objects referred to in the passage and describe how you think the Borrowers might have used them to make utensils, tools or furniture.

5 Have you lost anything recently? Describe how you set about looking for it and how your feelings changed as the search continued.

SPECIFIC SKILLS	additional comprehension questions; imaginative conjecture; descriptive and personal writing

The longest journey in the world

GENRE	poem
READING STRATEGIES	skimming; scanning; detailed reading
QUESTION FORM	questions requiring answers in complete sentences
UNDERSTANDING TESTED	question 5 - literal; questions 4, 7, 8 - deductive; questions 1, 2, 3, 6 - inferential

1 What was the game that the two boys played every night?
   They had a race to see who could get into their pyjamas and into bed first.
   The loser had to turn off the light. *(2 marks)*

2 Why was it so frightening to be the loser?
   The loser had to cross the room in darkness once he had turned off the light.
   The journey between light switch and bed was very frightening in the dark. *(2 marks)*

3 Why was it so wonderful to be the winner?
   It was wonderful to be the winner because you didn't have to switch off the light
   and cross the room in the dark. *(2 marks)*

4 Which verbs in the first verse suggest undressing very quickly?
   The verbs "ripping" and "kicking" suggest undressing at great speed. *(2 marks)*

5 What caused the moaning-moaning sound that could be heard in the room?
   It was the water in the water-pipes that made the moaning noise. *(1 mark)*

6 What was the boy really thinking each time he said, "I'm not scared"?
   He was trying to convince himself not to be scared, even though he really was. He was
   trying to think of sensible explanations for all the scary noises but he was still afraid. *(2 marks)*

7 What do you think the boy wasdoing while he said:
   "it takes so long / it takes so long / it takes so long"
   He wasmaking his way across the room in the dark with his heart beating. *(2 marks)*

8 What do you think the boy did at the words "to get there"?
   With these words he jumped into bed and felt safe. *(2 marks)*

Extension activities

1 Why do you think capital letters have been used in the last line of verse two and in the very last line of the poem?

2 Do you think the word "journey" is a good word to use to describe the distance from the light switch to the bed in this poem? Why?

3 Why is it a good idea to use such a vague word as "things" three times at the beginning of verse fo

4 Think carefully about the game that the boys play. Write out the rules very clearly so that there is no possibility of taking short cuts such as not putting on your pyjamas properly before getting into bed.

5 Describe how the boy feels at the end of the poem when he is safely in bed.

6 What could the parents of the boys do to stop them feeling so afraid? Make as many sensible suggestions as you can.

7 Have you ever felt frightened of the dark? Do you still feel frightened sometimes? Describe wh frightens you about the dark and how you cope.

SPECIFIC SKILLS	additional comprehension questions; writing rules; empathetic writing; giving advice; personal writing

Loll's first day

GENRE	fiction
READING STRATEGIES	skimming; scanning; detailed reading
QUESTION FORM	questions requiring answers in complete sentences
UNDERSTANDING TESTED	questions 3, 4, 5, 6, 8, 9, 11, 12 - deductive; questions 1, 2, 7, 10 - inferential

1 How did Loll feel about starting school?
He didn't want to go. (1 mark)

2 Who took him to school?
His sisters took him. (1 mark)

3 Why was he given a baked potato?
It was for his lunch. (1 mark)

4 Loll thought the story about the boy who didn't go to school was "overdoing it rather".
What does this mean?
It means that he thought it was a wild exaggeration just to frighten him. (2 marks)

5 Why did the playground "roar like a rodeo"?
The children were shouting as they rushed around. (1 mark)

6 Which word is the plural of "potato"?
"Potatoes" is the plural of "potato". (1 mark)

7 What did Loll think it meant when he was told to "sit there for the present"?
He thought it meant that he would get a gift in due course. (1 mark)

8 What did "sit there for the present" really mean?
It meant he should sit there just for the time being. (1 mark)

9 What sort of a temper is a "smouldering temper"?
It is one that goes on burning inside you but you keep mostly hidden. (2 marks)

10 Why did Loll go home in a smouldering temper?
Loll went home in a smouldering temper because he thought the promise of a gift had been broken. (1 mark)

11 After a week, Loll "felt like a veteran". What does this mean?
It means that he felt as though he had been going to school for a long time. (2 marks)

12 What does "ruthless" mean?
"Ruthless" means merciless. (1 mark)

Extension activities

1 What does "shrapnel" mean?

2 In what way was the grit of the playground like shrapnel?

3 What did the junior-teacher do when she "boxed a few ears"?

4 How did you feel when you went to school for the first time?
Describe your first day.

SPECIFIC SKILLS	additional comprehension questions; personal writing

Bad news

GENRE	classic children's fiction
READING STRATEGIES	skimming; scanning; detailed reading
QUESTION FORM	questions requiring answers in complete sentences
UNDERSTANDING TESTED	questions 3, 6, 7, 8 - deductive; questions 1, 2, 4 - inferential; question 5 - evaluative

1 Why did Ruth call the children's father the Master?
Ruth called him the Master because she was a servant in his household. (1 mark)

2 When Mother came back into the room, how could the children tell that she had heard some dreadful news?
They could tell from the expression on her face: she was very pale, her eyes were tearful and her mouth was sad. Also she seemed anxious to be left alone and hurried them off to bed. She said very little and was obviously trying to control herself. (3 marks)

3 "Roberta lingered to give Mother an extra hug." What does "lingered" mean?
It means she managed to be the last to leave the room by going slowly. (1 mark)

4 How could Roberta tell that her mother had been crying when she came to kiss them goodnight?
Roberta could tell from the way she was breathing that she had been crying. She was still catching her breath in a silent sob. (2 marks)

5 Roberta was the eldest child and Phyllis was the youngest. Would you guess this from the way they behave? Why?
Yes, Roberta was more mature and less self-centred. She quietly tried to comfort her mother with a hug but took the hint and left when she realised her mother wanted to be alone. She was more responsible than the other two and tried to stop them from gossiping and quarrelling. (4 marks)

6 What was Roberta's family nickname?
Her nickname was Bobbie. (1 mark)

7 What did Peter mean when he called Roberta "Miss Goody-Goody"?
He meant that she always tried to be so perfect and was always telling them what to do. (2 marks)

8 Roberta was sure that "some dire calamity" was happening. What does this mean?
It means she thought some terrible disaster was happening. (1 mark)

Extension activities

1 Think of at least three reasons why Mother interrupted Ruth at the beginning of the passage.

2 In what ways did Ruth speak differently from Mother and the children?

3 Why did Peter say he questioned Ruth?

4 When Ruth said "Don't ask me no questions and I won't tell you no lies", what did she mean?

5 The story that this passage comes from was publishedin 1906. What details in the passage show that it was written a long time ago?

SPECIFIC SKILLS	additional comprehension questions

Rosie and the boredom eater

GENRE	children's fiction
READING STRATEGIES	skimming; scanning; detailed reading
QUESTION FORM	questions requiring answers in complete sentences
NDERSTANDING TESTED	questions 1, 3, 4, 8 - literal; questions 5, 10 - deductive; questions 2, 6, 7 - inferential; question 9 - evaluative

1 Why was Rosie so bored?
She was bored because she had no one to play with and nothing to do. (1 mark)

2 What did Rosie mean when she said "there ought to be no such things as onlys"?
She thought no one should be an only child and everyone should have brothers and sisters. (2 marks)

3 What was the number of Rosie's new house and the name of the road?
Her house was 25 Latimer Street. (2 marks)

4 How could Rosie be sure that the house next door was empty?
She knew it was empty because the people who lived there had moved out weeks before. (1 mark)

5 The yard of the house next door was identical to Rosie's yard. What does "identical" mean?
"Identical" means "exactly the same". (1 mark)

6 Explain how Rosie knew that she wasn't in an earthquake when the dustbin started to rock about.
She knew she wasn't in an earthquake because nothing else was rocking about. (1 mark)

7 The old man in the dustbin said that he was there to help Rosie.
How do you think he will help her?
He is going to help her to get rid of boredom. (1 mark)

8 What facts do we learn about Rosie in this passage? (Look for information about her home, her family and her age.)
Her name is Rosie Barker. She is an only child. She lives at 25 Latimer Street. She is nine. (2 marks)

9 What do you find out about what Rosie's personality is like from this passage?
Include all the details that you can find.
She has a sense of humour. She is quite brave. She can be polite and she is good with words. She is lively. (3 marks)

10 What does "quavered" mean?
"Quavered" means "spoke with a wobbly voice". (1 mark)

Extension activities

1 Why did Rosie go into the yard of the house next door?

2 How Rosie was impertinent after her mother said she didn't want to hear the word "bored" again?

3 Imagine that Mrs Barker looks out of an upstairs window and sees Rosie in the yard next door. What do you think she would say to Rosie? Write her words.

4 Would you be bored in Rosie's situation without a garden and without any friends near by? What would you do?

5 In your opinion, what are the advantages and disadvantages of being a member of a large family?

SPECIFIC SKILLS	additional comprehension questions; writing in character; writing dialogue; expressing an opinion

Hop-scotch tots

GENRE	newspaper article
READING STRATEGIES	skimming; scanning; detailed reading
QUESTION FORM	questions requiring answers in complete sentences
UNDERSTANDING TESTED	questions 1, 2, 3, 4, 5, 7, 8 - literal; questions 9, 10 - deductive; question 6 - evaluative

1 How old are Katy and Hannah?
Katy and Hannah are four years old. (1 mark)

2 How far did the girls hop-scotch along Exmouth sea front?
They hop-scotched for a mile. (1 mark)

3 How much money did they raise?
They raised £350. (1 mark)

4 What must Katy not eat, drink or touch?
She must not eat or drink dairy products (such as butter, cheese, cream, milk) (1 mark)

5 What must Hannah not eat or touch?
She must not eat peanuts. (1 mark)

6 Their parents have to "watch them like a hawk". Why is this a good way of describing how they watch over the girls?
Hawks watch things with total concentration and do not miss anything that moves. They have very sharp eyes to see every detail. The girls' parents have to do the same thing. (1 mark)

7 List three possible allergic reactions the girls might have.
Accept 3 from: swelling, rashes, itchy spots, difficulty with breathing, a burning sensation. (2 marks)

8 If one of the girls did have an allergic reaction, what treatment should be used immediately?
Adrenaline should immediately be injected into a muscle. (1 mark)

9 How would the improved labelling of food help the girls?
Details about the ingredients would show which foods the girls could and could not eat. (1 mark)

10 What do the following words and phrases mean?
a) allergy - *means a condition in which a person becomes ill or uncomfortable when brought into contact with something that does not affect most people in the same way.*
b) vigilance - *means keeping careful watch at all times.*
c) product information - *means labelling food products to tell people what they contain.*
d) a medical breakthrough - *means an important new discovery of a medicine or a treatment*
e) legislation - *means making laws* (5 marks)

Extension activities

1 Read the title of the article again. In what ways is it a good title?

2 What would a sufferer from a food allergy gain from joining the Anaphylaxis Campaign?

3 Devise a booklet about food allergies for young children on behalf of the Anaphylaxis Campaign. Explain why some people should not eat certain foods, so that the message is clear without being frightening.

SPECIFIC SKILLS	additional questions; devising an information booklet

GENRE	children's fiction
READING STRATEGIES	skimming; scanning; detailed reading
QUESTION FORM	questions requiring answers in complete sentences
UNDERSTANDING TESTED	questions 1, 5, 6, 7, 8, 9, 10 - literal; questions 2, 4 - inferential; question 3 - evaluative

1 Barney's grandmother and his sister told him not to go too close to the edge of the
chalk-pit. What did they think might happen?
They thought the ground might collapse under his feet.   *(1 mark)*

2 What evidence in paragraph three shows that the edge of the chalk-pit was dangerous?
You could see where some of the ground under the trees has crumbled away.   *(2 marks)*

3 Which word best describes Barney's mood at the beginning of the passage?
(frightened excited bored)
"Bored" best describes Barney's mood.   *(2 marks)*

4 What was the local name for the chalk-pit?
The local name for the chalk-pit was the dump.   *(1 mark)*

5 What was growing at the very bottom of the pit?
Moss, elder and nettles were growing at the bottom of the pit.   *(1 mark)*

6 Why did Barney want to have the bicycle at the bottom of the pit?
He wanted it because he wasn't allowed to have one of his own.   *(2 marks)*

7 Explain in your own words the sound that Barney heard as he fell.
*He heard little bits of earth follow him down the pit, bouncing against the hard walls
and making a hard, dry sound.*   *(2 marks)*

8 What was the roof of the shelter made of?
The roof was made of elder branches, an old carpet and rusty old iron sheets.   *(1 mark)*

9 Why couldn't Barney move his legs?
He couldn't move his legs because they were caught up in the creeping plants.   *(2 marks)*

10 What did Barney think could have happened if he hadn't got tangled up in the plants?
He thought he could have broken his neck.   *(1 mark)*

Extension activities

1 What does "rickety" mean?

2 What is the difference between "holding" and "clutching"?

3 Make a list of all the plants and shrubs that are mentioned in the passage.

4 Barney is bored at the very beginning of the passage. Show how his mood changes several
times after that before the suspense at the end.

5 Barney is staying with his grandmother. Have you ever stayed at someone else's house?
Did it seem very different from living in your own house? Explain why.

SPECIFIC SKILLS	additional comprehension questions; writing a list; reflective writing; autobiographical writing

I am David

GENRE	children's fiction
READING STRATEGIES	skimming; scanning; detailed reading
QUESTION FORM	questions requiring answers in complete sentences
UNDERSTANDING TESTED	questions 2, 3, 5, 7, 8, 9, 10 - literal; question 6 - deductive; questions 1, 4 - inferential

1 Which words show that David had known the man for a long time?
   The words that show David had known the man for a long time are "David had known
   him all his life" and "David had known his name for as long as he could remember".   *(2 marks)*

2 What did David hate about the man's eyes?
   David hated the man's eyes because they were too small, pale and expressionless.   *(2 marks)*

3 Did David know the man's name?
   Yes, he had known it for as long as he could remember (but he never used it).   *(1 mark)*

4 Did David like the man?
   No, David hated him.   *(1 mark)*

5 How would David know that the electricity had been cut off?
   He would know the electricity had been cut off when he saw the man strike a match.   *(2 marks)*

6 How long would David have to climb over the wall?
   David would have thirty seconds to climb over the wall.   *(2 marks)*

7 What would David find hidden by the tree?
   David would find a compass and a bottle of water hidden by the tree.   *(2 marks)*

8 Where must David go first?
   He must go south to Salonica first.   *(1 mark)*

9 When he gets to Salonica, what must he do next?
   He must get on board a boat and hide.   *(1 mark)*

10 Why must David do his best to get to Denmark?
   He must do his best to get to Denmark because he will be safe there.   *(1 mark)*

Extension activities

1 Why did David have to wait for the electricity to be cut off before he climbed
   over the fence?

2 Why do you think the man was helping David?

3 What is a compass? Why did David need one?

4 What do the following underlined words mean?
   a) The man's eyes were repulsive.
   b) His face was gross and fat.
   c) David never spoke to him more than was barely necessary.
   d) The man had shrugged his shoulders.
   e) I don't know what my successor will decide to do about the job.

SPECIFIC SKILLS	additional comprehension questions; vocabulary

Key Comprehension Ginn & Co 1996. Copying permitted for purchasing school only. This material is not copyright free

Noise

GENRE	information text and bar chart
READING STRATEGIES	skimming; scanning; detailed reading
QUESTION FORM	questions requiring answers in complete sentences
UNDERSTANDING TESTED	questions 1, 2, 3, 4, 10, 11, 12 - literal; questions 5, 6, 7, 8, 9 - deductive; questions 13, 14 - inferential; question 15 - evaluative

1 Explain in your own words what effect noises of 180 decibels can have on rats.
   Rats might eat each other and have heart attacks if exposed to 180 decibels or more. (1 mark)

2 What effect can noises over 90 decibels have on a person?
   Noises over 90 decibels can hurt a person's ears and cause temporary deafness. (1 mark)

3 What should workers using pneumatic drills do to protect their ears from the noise?
   Workers using pneumatic drills should wear ear protection. (1 mark)

4 What is the noise level of a pneumatic drill if you are standing 1 metre away?
   The noise level of a pneumatic drill if you are standing 1 metre away is 120 decibels. (1 mark)

5 Which word in the passage means "lasting for a short time"?
   "Temporary" means "lasting for a short time". (1 mark)

6 Which word in the passage means "lasting for ever"?
   "Permanently" means "lasting for ever". (1 mark)

7 Which word in the passage means "stopped"?
   "Ceased" means "stopped". (1 mark)

8 Which word in the passage means "injury"?
   "Damage" means "injury". (1 mark)

9 Which word in the passage means "a buzzing in the ears"?
   "Tinnitus" means "a buzzing in the ears". (1 mark)

10 What is the decibel level of a normal conversation?
   The decibel level of a normal conversation is 60 decibels. (1 mark)

11 What is the decibel level of a ticking watch?
   A ticking watch makes a noise of 20 decibels. (1 mark)

12 Which item in the chart makes a noise of 100 decibels?
   A food mixer at 1 metre makes a noise of 100 decibels. (1 mark)

13 Which is noisier, the rustling of leaves in the wind or a whisper?
   A whisper is noisier. (1 mark)

14 Which is noisier, a pop group 1.5 metres away, or an accelerating motor cycle?
   A motor cycle is noisier. (1 mark)

15 Which decibel level surprises you most? Why?
   Reward any sensible answer logically justified. (1 mark)

Extension activities

1 Devise questions about the noise levels shown in the bar chart for a partner to answer.

2 Make a list of all the noises that you can hear in your classroom. Which of these sounds do you like best and which do you like least? Why?

SPECIFIC SKILLS	formulating and answering questions; making a list; expressing and justifying an opinion

Sam

GENRE	children's fiction
READING STRATEGIES	skimming; scanning; detailed reading
QUESTION FORM	questions requiring answers in complete sentences
UNDERSTANDING TESTED	questions 4, 6, 8 - literal; questions 2, 5, 7 - deductive; questions 1, 3, 9 - inferential; question 10 - evaluative

1 Why didn't Mrs Peach answer Sam when he spoke to her at first?
   Mrs Peach didn't answer because she was concentrating so much on preparing the dog food. (1 mark)

2 What is the difference between speaking and bellowing?
   Speaking means talking at a normal volume. Bellowing means shouting as loudly as you can. (2 marks)

3 Why did Sam look so brown?
   He looked so brown because he was very dirty. (1 mark)

4 How did Mrs Peach know that Sam was right when he said that it was Saturday?
   She realised that it must be Saturday because she remembered that the vet came the day before and he always came on a Friday. (1 mark)

5 What do you do if you groom a dog?
   If you groom a dog, you brush and clean it. (1 mark)

6 Mrs Peach was very forgetful. Write down four things that she forgot in this passage.
   She forgot what day it was. She forgots they had just had dinner. She forgot what she planned to do on Saturday. She forgot where her purse was. (2 marks)

7 "Sam spoke with an eye to his stomach." What does this mean?
   It means that he mentioned food because he was thinking about whether there was enough to eat in the house. He hoped Mrs Peach was planning to buy food. (1 mark)

8 Why was Mrs Peach's hair so untidy?
   It was untidy because she pushed her hand through it so often. (1 mark)

9 Why did Sam cross his fingers in the last paragraph?
   He crossed his fingers in case he had to tell his mother a lie. (Some people think that if you cross your fingers, it doesn't count as a lie.) (2 marks)

10 Do you think Mrs Peach was a good mother? Why?
   Reward any answer that is logically justified. (3 marks)

Extension activities

1 What were the advantages for Sam in having a mother like Mrs Peach?

2 What do the following words mean?
   a) resent
   b) omitted
   c) trifling
   d) conscientious
   e) perplexed

3 Write down five ways in which you think adults could be more considerate and five ways in which children could be more considerate.

SPECIFIC SKILLS	additional comprehension questions; vocabulary; personal writing